JUL   2009

U.S. PRESIDENTS

The
United States Presidents

GEORGE W. BUSH

ABDO Publishing Company

BreAnn Rumsch

visit us at
www.abdopublishing.com

Published by ABDO Publishing Company, 8000 West 78th Street, Edina, Minnesota 55439.
Copyright © 2009 by Abdo Consulting Group, Inc. International copyrights reserved in all
countries. No part of this book may be reproduced in any form without written permission from the
publisher. The Checkerboard Library™ is a trademark and logo of ABDO Publishing Company.

Printed in the United States.

Cover Photo: Corbis
Interior Photos: AP Images pp. 9, 11, 13, 14, 15, 16, 19, 21, 22, 23, 24, 26, 28; Corbis p. 18;
    Getty Images pp. 5, 17, 25, 27; iStockphoto p. 32

Editor: Megan M. Gunderson
Art Direction & Cover Design: Neil Klinepier
Interior Design: Neil Klinepier

Library of Congress Cataloging-in-Publication Data

Rumsch, BreAnn, 1981-
  George W. Bush / BreAnn Rumsch.
      p. cm. -- (The United States presidents)
  Includes index.
  ISBN 978-1-60453-444-3
  1. Bush, George W. (George Walker), 1946---Juvenile literature. 2. Presidents--United States--
Biography--Juvenile literature. I. Title.

  E903.R86 2009
  973.931092--dc22
  [B]
                              2008040272

CONTENTS

GEORGE W. BUSH

In 2001, George W. Bush became the forty-third president of the United States. The previous year, he had won one of the closest elections in U.S. history.

Before he became president, Bush grew up in Texas. After college, he served in the Texas **Air National Guard**. He also attended Harvard Business School. Bush then began his career in the oil industry. He later became an owner of the Texas Rangers baseball team.

In 1994, Texans elected Bush their governor. They reelected him in 1998. As governor, Bush improved education, cut taxes, and reformed the welfare system.

Republicans nominated Bush for president in 2000. He ran against Vice President Al Gore. The campaign was tough, and the election was close. It took weeks to determine the winner. Eventually, Bush claimed victory.

On January 20, 2001, Bush took office. Soon afterward, the United States faced the worst **terrorist** attacks in its history. After those attacks on September 11, 2001, Bush took immediate action to

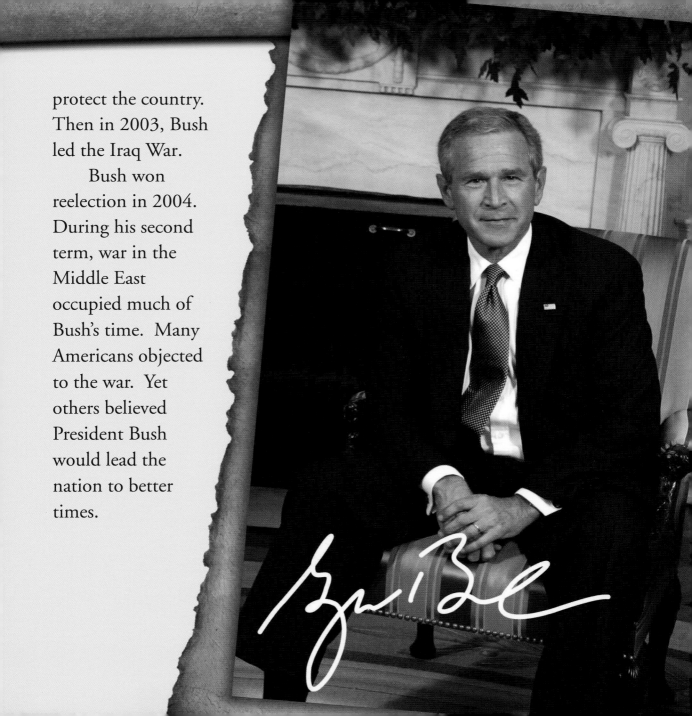

protect the country. Then in 2003, Bush led the Iraq War.

Bush won reelection in 2004. During his second term, war in the Middle East occupied much of Bush's time. Many Americans objected to the war. Yet others believed President Bush would lead the nation to better times.

TIMELINE

1946 - On July 6, George Walker Bush was born in New Haven, Connecticut.

1968 - Bush graduated from Yale University in New Haven; in July, Bush joined the Texas Air National Guard as a second lieutenant.

1973 - On October 1, Bush was honorably discharged from the Texas Air National Guard; Bush entered Harvard Business School in Boston, Massachusetts.

1975 - Bush graduated from Harvard.

1977 - Bush started Arbusto Energy; on November 5, Bush married Laura Lane Welch.

1989 - Bush became a partial owner of the Texas Rangers baseball team.

1994 - Bush was elected governor of Texas.

1998 - Bush was reelected governor.

2000 - Americans voted for president on November 7; on December 12, the U.S. Supreme Court stopped ballot recounts in Florida; Bush was declared the winner on December 13.

2001 - On January 20, Bush became the forty-third U.S. president; on September 11, terrorists attacked the United States; Bush ordered military attacks on Afghanistan; Bush created the Department of Homeland Security; Congress passed the USA Patriot Act.

2002 - Bush approved the No Child Left Behind Act.

2003 - In March, the Iraq War began; Bush signed the Medicare Act.

2005 - Bush began his second term as president; in August, Hurricane Katrina struck the Gulf Coast.

2008 - In February, Bush approved an economic stimulus package; March marked the fifth anniversary of the start of the Iraq War.

Did You Know?

In 2000, George W. Bush became the second son of a former president to be elected president himself. In 2004, he became the first son of a president to win reelection.

Bush received fewer popular votes than his opponent in the 2000 election. Yet, he won! This has happened to just three other presidents in U.S. history. They were John Quincy Adams in 1824, Rutherford B. Hayes in 1876, and Benjamin Harrison in 1888.

Throughout his life, Bush has had a number of nicknames. They include Junior, The Lip, Dubya, and Bushie.

In August 2008, Bush attended the Olympic Games in Beijing, China. He became the first U.S. president to attend the games in a foreign country.

YOUNG GEORGE

George Walker Bush was born in New Haven, Connecticut, on July 6, 1946. He was the first of Barbara and George H.W. Bush's six children. His sister Robin was born next. Jeb, Neil, Marvin, and Dorothy followed.

In 1948, George's family moved to Odessa, Texas. There, his father worked for an oil company. Two years later, the Bush family settled into a little blue house in Midland, Texas.

George spent his childhood in Midland. There, he played with the children in his neighborhood. They liked to ride their bicycles and play marbles and baseball.

Sadly, George's little sister Robin died of **cancer** in 1953. Her death troubled George for a long time. His parents were heartbroken, too. Young George tried to cheer them up by telling jokes and playing games.

FAST FACTS

BORN - July 6, 1946
WIFE - Laura Lane Welch (1946–)
CHILDREN - 2
POLITICAL PARTY - Republican
AGE AT INAUGURATION - 54
YEARS SERVED - 2001–2009
VICE PRESIDENT - Dick Cheney

Young George (center) *with his parents*

Later, George attended San Jacinto Junior High School in Midland. He was an average student. Yet, he was elected class president. He also played quarterback on San Jacinto's football team.

SCHOOL DAYS

Meanwhile, George's father traveled much for work. Eventually, his company began drilling for oil in the Gulf of Mexico. So, he moved his business to be near the Gulf. In 1959, the Bushes settled in Houston, Texas. George transferred to a private school there called the Kincaid School.

George's parents wanted him to have the best education possible. So in 1961, they sent him to Phillips Academy in Andover, Massachusetts. George missed his family and struggled with his lessons. He feared he might fail.

However, George decided to try his best. He stayed up late studying. He also made many new friends. George played on the baseball and basketball teams. And, he became the head football cheerleader his senior year.

In 1964, George graduated from Phillips Academy. That fall, he entered Yale University in New Haven, Connecticut. At Yale, George studied history. He also played baseball and rugby. In addition, George loved to be social. So, he joined a **fraternity** and was elected its president.

George's love of baseball began at a young age. It has stayed with him throughout his life.

FLIGHT SCHOOL

Bush graduated from Yale in 1968. He then joined the Texas **Air National Guard**. In July, he entered as a second lieutenant. Bush went to Lackland Air Force Base in San Antonio, Texas. There, he participated in basic training.

That November, Bush entered flight school at Moody Air Force Base in Valdosta, Georgia. He graduated in 1969. His father gave a speech at the graduation ceremony.

In December, Bush left for Ellington Air Force Base in Houston. There, he learned to fly F-102 fighter airplanes. On June 23, Bush finished his combat flight training. He graduated with the rank of lieutenant.

After graduation, Bush continued flying for the Texas Air National Guard part-time. He also had several other jobs. First, he worked for an agricultural company. Then, he worked on Alabama **Republican** William Blount's campaign for U.S. Senate. He also got a job working with poor children in Houston.

Bush eventually decided to return to school. On October 1, 1973, he was honorably discharged from the Texas **Air National Guard**. He then entered Harvard Business School in Boston, Massachusetts.

Bush was assigned to the 147th Fighter-Interceptor Group at Moody Air Force Base.

BUSINESS AND POLITICS

Mr. and Mrs. Bush (center) *on their wedding day with Bush's parents*

In 1975, Bush graduated from Harvard Business School. He wanted to work in the oil business like his father. So, he returned to his childhood home of Midland, Texas.

There, Bush first worked as a "landman." He looked up land titles at the county records office. The titles showed him who owned what land.

14

Then, Bush contacted the landowners. He asked them if oil companies could rent the land to drill for oil.

In 1977, Bush started his own oil company. He called it Arbusto Energy. That same year, Bush met school librarian Laura Lane Welch. On November 5, the couple married. Four years later, the Bushes welcomed twin girls. They named their daughters Jenna and Barbara.

Jenna (left) *and Barbara helped their father campaign for presidential reelection in 2004.*

In 1978, Bush campaigned for support from workers in the Texas oil fields.

Meanwhile, Bush had decided to enter politics. In 1978, he campaigned for a seat in the U.S. House of Representatives. Bush ran as a **Republican**. His opponent was **Democrat** Kent Hance.

Hance claimed Bush was an outsider. He reminded Texan voters that Bush had been born and educated outside of Texas. So, Bush lost the election.

After his defeat, Bush returned to Arbusto Energy. He raised money from investors to build his business. In 1982, Bush changed the company's name to Bush Exploration.

By this time, the oil industry was in trouble. Oil prices were dropping, and Bush Exploration was losing money. So in 1984, Bush sold his company to Spectrum Corporation.

Meanwhile, the oil industry continued to struggle. Bush knew Spectrum needed help. In 1986, the Harken Oil and Gas company agreed to buy Spectrum. Bush took a job at Harken as a consultant. He also served on the board of directors.

In 1988, Bush's father ran for president. Bush helped with the campaign. He worked as an adviser and a speechwriter. Bush's father easily won the election.

That same year, Bush learned that the Texas Rangers baseball team was for sale. He organized a group of investors. Together, they bought the team in 1989.

Bush enjoyed being a team owner. As managing general partner, he promoted the Rangers. Bush also worked to increase attendance at games. Soon, he won support to build a new baseball stadium for the team.

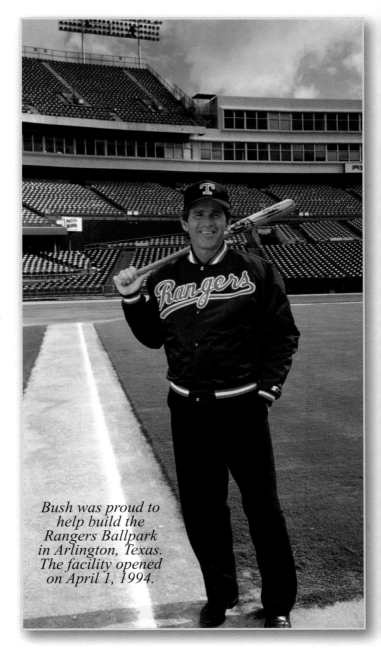

Bush was proud to help build the Rangers Ballpark in Arlington, Texas. The facility opened on April 1, 1994.

GOVERNOR BUSH

Bush campaigned hard to win over Texans.

Bush focused on his work, but he was still interested in politics. So in 1994, he ran for governor of Texas. His opponent was Governor Ann Richards.

The campaign was difficult. Richards claimed Bush was unqualified for the job. However, Bush focused on what he thought was best for Texas. He promised to lower crime rates and increase spending on education. He also pledged to reform the welfare system. Texans liked Bush's ideas. That year, he won the election.

As governor, Bush improved public education and increased teacher salaries. He made sure people in the welfare system fulfilled work requirements. Governor Bush supported bills for tougher punishment of juvenile criminals. He also reduced property taxes.

Bush ran for reelection in 1998. His opponent was Texas land **commissioner** Garry Mauro. Texans still liked Bush. He had kept many of his campaign promises during his first term. So, he won the election in a landslide.

Governor Bush's work made him nationally known. So in August 2000, the **Republican** Party chose him to run for president. Bush chose former **secretary of defense** Dick Cheney as his **running mate**. The **Democratic** Party nominated Vice President Al Gore. Gore's running mate was Connecticut senator Joseph Lieberman.

Vice President Dick Cheney served as secretary of defense when Bush's father was president.

THE 2000 ELECTION

During his campaign for president, Bush traveled across the country. He promised Americans he would reform education, cut taxes, and improve **Social Security**.

Americans voted on November 7, 2000. It proved to be one of America's closest elections. To win, a candidate needed to earn at least 270 Electoral College votes. But at the end of the night, neither candidate had won enough electoral votes.

Florida's votes had yet to be assigned. Whoever won the state's 25 electoral votes would become president. Yet, Florida's results remained too close to call. There, Bush had beaten Gore by only a few hundred **popular votes**. Florida law says if an election is that close, the **ballots** must be recounted by machine. Four days later, the recount showed Bush was still in the lead.

Gore wanted some of the ballots recounted by hand. Florida permitted the recount. But Bush felt this was unfair. So, he filed **lawsuits** in state and federal courts. Bush lost these lawsuits, so he appealed to the U.S. **Supreme Court**.

The **Supreme Court** made its final decision on December 12. It stopped all hand recounts in Florida. As a result, Florida's electoral votes were awarded to Bush. This was the only election decided by the Supreme Court.

Gore had won more **popular votes** nationwide. But now Bush had 271 electoral votes to Gore's 266. On December 13, Gore **conceded** the election to Bush.

Al Gore

DETERMINED LEADER

Bush was inaugurated outside of the U.S. Capitol.

On January 20, 2001, Bush was **inaugurated** the forty-third U.S. president. Immediately, he began working hard for Americans.

Bush soon faced a challenge unlike any other. On September 11, 2001, **terrorists** carried out surprise attacks against the United States. They intentionally crashed airplanes in New York, Washington, D.C., and Pennsylvania. These acts caused much damage and killed about 3,000 people.

Bush vowed that fighting **terrorism** would be his top priority as president. That night he said, "None of us will ever forget this day. Yet, we go forward to defend freedom and all that is good and just in our world."

The United States quickly learned that **al-Qaeda** was behind the attacks. The group was located in Afghanistan. Its leader was a terrorist named Osama bin Laden.

Bush stopped to encourage rescue workers while touring the destruction following the September 11 attacks.

President Bush spoke with Afghanistan's government, the Taliban. He asked the Taliban to turn over bin Laden and shut down al-Qaeda. But the Taliban refused. So on October 7, Bush ordered military attacks on Afghanistan. After 11 weeks of war, the Taliban was defeated. However, bin Laden was not captured during the conflict.

Meanwhile, President Bush worked hard to improve the lives of Americans at home. In October 2001, he created the Department of Homeland Security. It became responsible for protecting the United States from further attacks.

On October 26, 2001, Bush signed the USA Patriot Act.

That same month, Congress passed the USA Patriot Act. This law helped agencies such as the Federal Bureau of Investigation (FBI). The act gave FBI agents more freedom to search for suspected **terrorists**.

Bush also worked to reform education and health care. In 2002, he approved the No Child Left Behind Act. It encouraged schools to help students improve their test scores. The next year, Bush signed the Medicare Act of 2003. For the first time, elderly Americans would get help paying for medication.

Then in March 2003, the Iraq War began. Bush believed Iraqi president Saddam Hussein was a threat to America's security. So, the United States launched an attack on Iraq. Most Americans supported Bush's decision to invade Iraq.

Soon, the Iraqi government fell. In May, President Bush declared that major combat operations there had ended. However, U.S. troops remained in Iraq to help the new government maintain control.

U.S. forces captured Saddam Hussein in Iraq on December 13, 2003.

Soon, the U.S. government's **debt** grew from paying for the war. By 2004, many Americans no longer believed the war was a good idea.

TOUGH TIMES

As the war continued, President Bush and Vice President Cheney faced reelection. In 2004, the **Democrats** nominated Massachusetts senator John Kerry for president. His **running mate** was North Carolina senator John Edwards.

The campaign was long and difficult. On election day, more

Bush and Kerry (right)

than 115 million Americans voted. It was the highest voter turnout since 1968! Bush defeated Kerry by only a small lead. Bush earned 286 electoral votes to Kerry's 252 votes.

President Bush began his second term on January 20, 2005. That August, **Hurricane** Katrina struck the Gulf Coast. About 1,800 people died because of the storm. The

SUPREME COURT APPOINTMENTS

JOHN G. ROBERTS JR. - 2005
SAMUEL A. ALITO - 2006

26

On September 2, 2005, Bush signed a relief bill. It was the first of several to help the Gulf Coast recover from Hurricane Katrina.

hurricane left thousands homeless. Bush sent aid to the region. But, many people were upset because rescue operations were delayed.

In 2007, the Iraq War was still raging. Bush wanted to send more troops to Iraq. But Congress disagreed. Instead, Congress passed a bill requiring Bush to begin withdrawing troops. On May 1, Bush **vetoed** the bill. He believed withdrawing troops would put all the military's hard work at risk.

President Bush is grateful for the service of those in the nation's armed forces.

Meanwhile, the **economy** was in trouble. By late 2007, many people had lost their jobs. The **cost of living** was increasing. At the same time, home values were falling. Some people could no longer afford their house payments.

So in February 2008, President Bush approved an economic stimulus package. It returned some money to taxpayers and businesses. By spending this money, Americans could help boost the economy. That March marked the fifth anniversary of the start of the Iraq War. Leaders hoped the nation would soon be able to stand on its own.

Bush left the White House in January 2009. Plans for the George W. Bush Presidential Center are in progress. The center will be located at Southern Methodist University in Dallas, Texas.

George W. Bush faced many challenges as president. He fought **terrorism** at home and in foreign lands. He also struggled to improve a slowing economy. Many Americans questioned Bush's decisions. But, he always did what he believed was best for the nation.

PRESIDENT BUSH'S CABINET

FIRST TERM
JANUARY 20, 2001– JANUARY 20, 2005

- **STATE** – Colin Powell
- **TREASURY** – Paul O'Neill
  John Snow (from February 3, 2003)
- **ATTORNEY GENERAL** – John Ashcroft
- **INTERIOR** – Gale Norton
- **AGRICULTURE** – Ann M. Veneman
- **COMMERCE** – Don Evans
- **LABOR** – Elaine Chao
- **DEFENSE** – Donald Rumsfeld
- **HEALTH AND HUMAN SERVICES** –
  Tommy Thompson
- **HOUSING AND URBAN DEVELOPMENT** –
  Mel Martinez
  Alphonso Jackson (from April 1, 2004)
- **TRANSPORTATION** – Norman Mineta
- **ENERGY** – Spencer Abraham
- **EDUCATION** – Rod Paige
- **VETERANS AFFAIRS** – Anthony Principi
- **HOMELAND SECURITY** –
  Tom Ridge (from October 8, 2001)

SECOND TERM
JANUARY 20, 2005– JANUARY 20, 2009

- **STATE** – Colin Powell, Condoleezza Rice (from January 26, 2005)
- **TREASURY** – John Snow, Henry M. Paulson Jr. (from July 10, 2006)
- **ATTORNEY GENERAL** – John Ashcroft
  Alberto Gonzales (from February 3, 2005)
  Michael B. Mukasey (from November 9, 2007)
- **INTERIOR** – Gale Norton
  Dirk Kempthorne (from May 26, 2006)
- **AGRICULTURE** – Ann M. Veneman
  Mike Johanns (from January 21, 2005)
- **COMMERCE** – Don Evans, Carlos Gutierrez (from February 7, 2005)
- **LABOR** – Elaine Chao
- **DEFENSE** – Donald Rumsfeld, Robert Gates (from December 18, 2006)
- **HEALTH AND HUMAN SERVICES** – Tommy Thompson
  Michael O. Leavitt (from January 26, 2005)
- **HOUSING AND URBAN DEVELOPMENT** – Alphonso Jackson
- **TRANSPORTATION** – Norman Mineta
- **ENERGY** – Spencer Abraham
  Samuel W. Bodman (from February 1, 2005)
- **EDUCATION** – Margaret Spellings
- **VETERANS AFFAIRS** – Anthony Principi
  Jim Nicholson (from February 1, 2005)
- **HOMELAND SECURITY** – Tom Ridge
  Michael Chertoff (from February 15, 2005)

OFFICE OF THE PRESIDENT

BRANCHES OF GOVERNMENT

The U.S. government is divided into three branches. They are the executive, legislative, and judicial branches. This division is called a separation of powers. Each branch has some power over the others. This is called a system of checks and balances.

EXECUTIVE BRANCH

The executive branch enforces laws. It is made up of the president, the vice president, and the president's cabinet. The president represents the United States around the world. He or she oversees relations with other countries and signs treaties. The president signs bills into law and appoints officials and federal judges. He or she also leads the military and manages government workers.

LEGISLATIVE BRANCH

The legislative branch makes laws, maintains the military, and regulates trade. It also has the power to declare war. This branch consists of the Senate and the House of Representatives. Together, these two houses make up Congress. Each state has two senators. A state's population determines the number of representatives it has.

JUDICIAL BRANCH

The judicial branch interprets laws. It consists of district courts, courts of appeals, and the Supreme Court. District courts try cases. If a person disagrees with a trial's outcome, he or she may appeal. If the courts of appeals support the ruling, a person may appeal to the Supreme Court. The Supreme Court also makes sure that laws follow the U.S. Constitution.

Qualifications for Office

To be president, a person must meet three requirements. A candidate must be at least 35 years old and a natural-born U.S. citizen. He or she must also have lived in the United States for at least 14 years.

Electoral College

The U.S. presidential election is an indirect election. Voters from each state choose electors to represent them in the Electoral College. The number of electors from each state is based on population. Each elector has one electoral vote. Electors are pledged to cast their vote for the candidate who receives the highest number of popular votes in their state. A candidate must receive the majority of Electoral College votes to win.

Term of Office

Each president may be elected to two four-year terms. Sometimes, a president may only be elected once. This happens if he or she served more than two years of the previous president's term.

The presidential election is held on the Tuesday after the first Monday in November. The president is sworn in on January 20 of the following year. At that time, he or she takes the oath of office:

I do solemnly swear (or affirm) that I will faithfully execute the office of President of the United States, and will to the best of my ability, preserve, protect and defend the Constitution of the United States.

LINE OF SUCCESSION

The Presidential Succession Act of 1947 defines who becomes president if the president cannot serve. The vice president is first in the line of succession. Next are the Speaker of the House and the President Pro Tempore of the Senate. If none of these individuals is able to serve, the office falls to the president's cabinet members. They would take office in the order in which each department was created:

| Secretary of State |
| Secretary of the Treasury |
| Secretary of Defense |
| Attorney General |
| Secretary of the Interior |
| Secretary of Agriculture |
| Secretary of Commerce |
| Secretary of Labor |
| Secretary of Health and Human Services |
| Secretary of Housing and Urban Development |
| Secretary of Transportation |
| Secretary of Energy |
| Secretary of Education |
| Secretary of Veterans Affairs |
| Secretary of Homeland Security |

Benefits

• While in office, the president receives a salary of $400,000 each year. He or she lives in the White House and has 24-hour Secret Service protection.

• The president may travel on a Boeing 747 jet called Air Force One. The airplane can accommodate 70 passengers. It has kitchens, a dining room, sleeping areas, and a conference room. It also has fully equipped offices with the latest communications systems. Air Force One can fly halfway around the world before needing to refuel. It can even refuel in flight!

• If the president wishes to travel by car, he or she uses Cadillac One. Cadillac One is a Cadillac Deville. It has been modified with heavy armor and communications systems. The president takes Cadillac One along when visiting other countries if secure transportation will be needed.

• The president also travels on a helicopter called Marine One. Like the presidential car, Marine One accompanies the president when traveling abroad if necessary.

• Sometimes, the president needs to get away and relax with family and friends. Camp David is the official presidential retreat. It is located in the cool, wooded mountains in Maryland. The U.S. Navy maintains the retreat, and the U.S. Marine Corps keeps it secure. The camp offers swimming, tennis, golf, and hiking.

• When the president leaves office, he or she receives Secret Service protection for ten more years. He or she also receives a yearly pension of $191,300 and funding for office space, supplies, and staff.

PRESIDENTS AND THEIR TERMS

PRESIDENT	PARTY	TOOK OFFICE	LEFT OFFICE	TERMS SERVED	VICE PRESIDENT
George Washington	None	April 30, 1789	March 4, 1797	Two	John Adams
John Adams	Federalist	March 4, 1797	March 4, 1801	One	Thomas Jefferson
Thomas Jefferson	Democratic-Republican	March 4, 1801	March 4, 1809	Two	Aaron Burr, George Clinton
James Madison	Democratic-Republican	March 4, 1809	March 4, 1817	Two	George Clinton, Elbridge Gerry
James Monroe	Democratic-Republican	March 4, 1817	March 4, 1825	Two	Daniel D. Tompkins
John Quincy Adams	Democratic-Republican	March 4, 1825	March 4, 1829	One	John C. Calhoun
Andrew Jackson	Democrat	March 4, 1829	March 4, 1837	Two	John C. Calhoun, Martin Van Buren
Martin Van Buren	Democrat	March 4, 1837	March 4, 1841	One	Richard M. Johnson
William H. Harrison	Whig	March 4, 1841	April 4, 1841	Died During First Term	John Tyler
John Tyler	Whig	April 6, 1841	March 4, 1845	Completed Harrison's Term	Office Vacant
James K. Polk	Democrat	March 4, 1845	March 4, 1849	One	George M. Dallas
Zachary Taylor	Whig	March 5, 1849	July 9, 1850	Died During First Term	Millard Fillmore

PRESIDENT	PARTY	TOOK OFFICE	LEFT OFFICE	TERMS SERVED	VICE PRESIDENT
Millard Fillmore	Whig	July 10, 1850	March 4, 1853	Completed Taylor's Term	Office Vacant
Franklin Pierce	Democrat	March 4, 1853	March 4, 1857	One	William R.D. King
James Buchanan	Democrat	March 4, 1857	March 4, 1861	One	John C. Breckinridge
Abraham Lincoln	Republican	March 4, 1861	April 15, 1865	Served One Term, Died During Second Term	Hannibal Hamlin, Andrew Johnson
Andrew Johnson	Democrat	April 15, 1865	March 4, 1869	Completed Lincoln's Second Term	Office Vacant
Ulysses S. Grant	Republican	March 4, 1869	March 4, 1877	Two	Schuyler Colfax, Henry Wilson
Rutherford B. Hayes	Republican	March 3, 1877	March 4, 1881	One	William A. Wheeler
James A. Garfield	Republican	March 4, 1881	September 19, 1881	Died During First Term	Chester Arthur
Chester Arthur	Republican	September 20, 1881	March 4, 1885	Completed Garfield's Term	Office Vacant
Grover Cleveland	Democrat	March 4, 1885	March 4, 1889	One	Thomas A. Hendricks
Benjamin Harrison	Republican	March 4, 1889	March 4, 1893	One	Levi P. Morton
Grover Cleveland	Democrat	March 4, 1893	March 4, 1897	One	Adlai E. Stevenson
William McKinley	Republican	March 4, 1897	September 14, 1901	Served One Term, Died During Second Term	Garret A. Hobart, Theodore Roosevelt

PRESIDENT	PARTY	TOOK OFFICE	LEFT OFFICE	TERMS SERVED	VICE PRESIDENT
Theodore Roosevelt	Republican	September 14, 1901	March 4, 1909	Completed McKinley's Second Term, Served One Term	Office Vacant, Charles Fairbanks
William Taft	Republican	March 4, 1909	March 4, 1913	One	James S. Sherman
Woodrow Wilson	Democrat	March 4, 1913	March 4, 1921	Two	Thomas R. Marshall
Warren G. Harding	Republican	March 4, 1921	August 2, 1923	Died During First Term	Calvin Coolidge
Calvin Coolidge	Republican	August 3, 1923	March 4, 1929	Completed Harding's Term, Served One Term	Office Vacant, Charles Dawes
Herbert Hoover	Republican	March 4, 1929	March 4, 1933	One	Charles Curtis
Franklin D. Roosevelt	Democrat	March 4, 1933	April 12, 1945	Served Three Terms, Died During Fourth Term	John Nance Garner, Henry A. Wallace, Harry S. Truman
Harry S. Truman	Democrat	April 12, 1945	January 20, 1953	Completed Roosevelt's Fourth Term, Served One Term	Office Vacant, Alben Barkley
Dwight D. Eisenhower	Republican	January 20, 1953	January 20, 1961	Two	Richard Nixon
John F. Kennedy	Democrat	January 20, 1961	November 22, 1963	Died During First Term	Lyndon B. Johnson
Lyndon B. Johnson	Democrat	November 22, 1963	January 20, 1969	Completed Kennedy's Term, Served One Term	Office Vacant, Hubert H. Humphrey
Richard Nixon	Republican	January 20, 1969	August 9, 1974	Completed First Term, Resigned During Second Term	Spiro T. Agnew, Gerald Ford

PRESIDENT	PARTY	TOOK OFFICE	LEFT OFFICE	TERMS SERVED	VICE PRESIDENT
Gerald Ford	Republican	August 9, 1974	January 20, 1977	Completed Nixon's Second Term	Nelson A. Rockefeller
Jimmy Carter	Democrat	January 20, 1977	January 20, 1981	One	Walter Mondale
Ronald Reagan	Republican	January 20, 1981	January 20, 1989	Two	George H.W. Bush
George H.W. Bush	Republican	January 20, 1989	January 20, 1993	One	Dan Quayle
Bill Clinton	Democrat	January 20, 1993	January 20, 2001	Two	Al Gore
George W. Bush	Republican	January 20, 2001	January 20, 2009	Two	Dick Cheney
Barack Obama	Democrat	January 20, 2009			Joe Biden

"We seek peace. We strive for peace. And sometimes peace must be defended." George W. Bush

WRITE TO THE PRESIDENT

You may write to the president at:

**The White House
1600 Pennsylvania Avenue NW
Washington, DC 20500**

You may e-mail the president at:
comments@whitehouse.gov

GLOSSARY

Air National Guard - U.S. air defense units commanded by individual state governors as well as the president. They are trained to promptly mobilize during war and to provide assistance during national emergencies.

al-Qaeda (al KEYE-duh) - an Islamic organization founded by Osama bin Laden. It opposes the presence of the United States and other foreign nations in Islamic lands. The organization trains its followers and engages in acts of terrorism around the world.

ballot - a piece of paper used to cast a vote.

cancer - any of a group of often deadly diseases characterized by an abnormal growth of cells that destroys healthy tissues and organs.

commissioner - an official in charge of a government department.

concede - to admit something. Political candidates concede defeat after they have lost an election.

cost of living - the average cost of goods and services necessary to maintain the standard lifestyle. In countries with a high cost of living, goods and services are expensive.

debt - something owed to someone, usually money.

Democrat - a member of the Democratic political party. Democrats believe in social change and strong government.

economy - the way a nation uses its money, goods, and natural resources.

fraternity - a social, professional, or honorary society for males, especially college students. Names of these student organizations are typically combinations of letters from the Greek alphabet.

hurricane - a tropical storm with strong, circular winds, rain, thunder, and lightning.

inaugurate (ih-NAW-gyuh-rayt) - to swear into a political office.

lawsuit - a case held before a court.

popular vote - the vote of the entire body of people with the right to vote.

Republican - a member of the Republican political party. Republicans are conservative and believe in small government.

running mate - a candidate running for a lower-rank position on an election ticket, especially the candidate for vice president.

secretary of defense - a member of the president's cabinet who directs the operations of the nation's armed forces and advises the president on military matters.

Social Security - a national pension program established by the U.S. government in 1935. The program provides aid to those in need, such as the elderly, children, and disabled people. The system is funded through employer and employee contributions.

Supreme Court - the highest, most powerful court in the United States.

terrorism - the use of terror, violence, or threats to frighten people into action. A person who commits an act of terrorism is called a terrorist.

veto - the right of one member of a decision-making group to stop an action by the group. In the U.S. government, the president can veto bills passed by Congress. But Congress can override the president's veto if two-thirds of its members vote to do so.

WEB SITES

To learn more about George W. Bush, visit ABDO Publishing Company on the World Wide Web at **www.abdopublishing.com**. Web sites about George W. Bush are featured on our Book Links page. These links are routinely monitored and updated to provide the most current information available.

INDEX